RED–BLACK CONNECTION
Contemporary Urban African-Native Americans
and Their Stories of Dual Identity

Valena Broussard Dismukes

Grace Enterprises
Los Angeles, California

Library of Congress PCN 2007903178

Dismukes, Valena Broussard, 1938–
The Red-Black Connection: Contemporary Urban African Native Americans and their Stories of Dual Identity.
Fifty-two photographs and narratives with ten additional photographs.
Includes bibliographical references, history and additional resources

1. African-Americans – United States.
2. American Indians – United States.
3. Racial Identity – United States.
4. Mixed Bloods – United States.
5. Black Indians – United States
6. Title

Copyright © 2007 by Valena Broussard Dismukes
Grace Enterprises GE
3800 Stocker St., Suite 1
Los Angeles, California 90008
Inquiries: vdismukes@netzero.net

All rights reserved. No part of this book may be reproduced or transmitted in any form, by any means, electronic or mechanical, including photocopying, recording, or by any information storage and retrieval system, without permission in writing from the author, except for the inclusion of brief quotations in a review.

Printed in USA by Mira Digital Publishing.
ISBN 978-0-9797153-0-3

Cover photograph by the author
Author's photograph by Michael Ramon Dismukes
Cover and book design by Marsha H. Levine

IN MEMORY OF

Zenobia Embry-Nimmer

Susie Gerrard

Wilmer James

Georgia Joseph

James Howard Scott

My African ancestors from Sierra Leone

My Choctaw ancestors from Mississippi

ACKNOWLEDGEMENTS

The photographic essay, "Native Americans: The Red-Black Connection," on which this book is based would not have been possible without the support of members of the African/American Indian community. Their willingness to share their stories with the public took great courage. Other, heretofore silent, members of the African-American community have been encouraged to step forward and lay claim to their often-shrouded Indian histories. As a result, the general public has been exposed to new ideas and information that have challenged what it has been taught about American Indians.

James Burks, director of the William Grant Still Art Center in Los Angeles, nurtured the celebration of the Diaspora of Africans at the Los Angeles African Marketplace. With the addition of a powwow to this annual event, the project gained impetus.

There are those along the path of my exploration who played a role in the development of the photographic essay and who have greatly enriched my life; members of both the African-American and American Indian communities who demonstrated interest and support; Kat High (Hupa), documentary videographer, who embraced my project and featured it on her Adelphia access TV program; Rose Figueroa (Apache) who curated the exhibit at the Southwest Museum, an institution devoted to the history and culture of American Indians; Silver Lab for its photo printing and donation of sepia toning for the traveling exhibit; and finally, my son, Michael, who asked me, "What are you going to do with the second half of your life?"

Thanks also go to a cadre of people that helped to propel my photographic essay into book form: Isa Kae Meksin and Margo O'Connell, who first suggested that the work should be put into book form; S. Pearl Sharp for her helpful comments and encouragement; Dan McCory for his editing; Jim Pieper for his valuable advice; and Anita Harrell for her review of the history section. Any errors or omissions that appear in this work are strictly of my own doing.

> **"You can't tell who people are by merely looking at them."**
>
> —
>
> *Jack Forbes, Ph.D., Professor, University of California, Davis*
> *Lecture, Southwest Museum, Los Angeles, California, 1998*

TABLE OF CONTENTS

Introduction	x
Photographs and narratives	1
Additional photographs	69
Afterword	76
Appendixes	77
A. Bibliography	77
B. Related Resources	78
C. Historical Overview	84
D. Historic Red-Black People	88
E. Musings	89

PREFACE

Since the days of the arrival in the Western Hemisphere of Columbus and others sailing under the Spanish flag, the lives of Africans and Native American Indians have been intertwined. Enslaved Africans escaping Spanish control would flee to the woods where friendly Indians harbored them. A common enemy, similar cultures, and later, intermarriage linked these two groups. The marriages were usually between African men and Indian women.

The European introduction of slavery of both groups brought them together into increased contact, especially along the eastern seaboard and the southeastern colonies. By the mid 1800's, there were an estimated four million Red-Black people in the colonies.

Southeastern nations (Cherokee, Choctaw, Creek, Chickasaw, and Seminoles, to a lesser degree) modeled themselves after the European colonists and often became owners of African slaves. The mixture of male Indian slave owners and female African slaves added a new layer to the issue of slavery and ethnicity in America.

According to the 2004 census, more than 1,800,000 individuals identified themselves as being of African and Indian descent. This number is a conservative one and does not accurately reflect the estimated 20 million African Americans who have Indian ancestry.

Today, more and more African-Americans are researching their oral and written history, participating in traditional powwows, and claiming the Indian heritage that is their birthright.

INTRODUCTION

As a young girl growing up in Missouri, I heard my family discuss our Indian heritage casually and only upon occasion. We had very little information about our forebears in Mississippi. It was not until I was an adult living in Los Angeles that it was revealed that an ancestor was believed to have been a signer of the Dancing Rabbit Creek Treaty of 1831. It was this treaty between the United States government and the Choctaw nation that lead to the removal of a majority the Choctaws from Mississippi into Oklahoma. A land allotment due us was never received.

For many years, I have been involved in things Indian, participating in political protests, bringing an Indian perspective into my classroom, and attending powwows. It was during a powwow in 1996 that I was struck by the greatly increased presence of dark-skinned Indians, apparently with some trace of African blood, dancing in the arena. "Who are these people?" I asked. "How and why have they stepped into this public space? What are the issues surrounding their claim to Indian ancestry?"

It was this observation that began my inquiry into people of African and Indian descent. Adding fuel to this curiosity was my attendance at the first African Marketplace Powwow in 1997 and the Southwest Museum lecture on Red-Black people in 1998. Thus was born the idea of the photographic essay, "Native Americans—The Red-Black Connection" on which this book is based. It was to be, I thought, just a wonderful way for me to investigate the topic and gain new insights into culture. With a survey upon which to base interviews, and armed with my trusty Nikon, I talked with friends, dancers, and spectators at powwows, and just about anyone who looked as though they shared this dual heritage.

One of the first challenges was to decide on the term to be used to describe this population. The term "Black Indians" was used for the title of William Katz' 1986 book on the subject. Jack Forbes, on the other hand, subtitled his 1993 book, "The Language of Race and the Evolution of Red-Black People." Other terms frequently used are Afro-Indian, African Indians, African/Native Americans, or more simply, Indians. I settled on the term Red-Black because I believed it appropriately acknowledged the duality of the heritage and served as a useful shorthand in the discussion of a complex history.

I spent many months over several years photographing and collecting information from people in California, Oklahoma, and New Hampshire. They represented tribes from many areas of the country. Some of those interviewed knew they had Indian ancestors but had very little information about their histories. Others were involved in genealogical research and expressed an interest in learning more about Indian culture and history. An interest in the history, however, did not always indicate an interest in identifying as Indian. Several held to spiritual beliefs combining Indian, African, and in some cases, Asian systems. Most felt a common bond with Indians as fellow members of oppressed minorities in the United States.

Few contemporary African-Americans speak publicly about the need for political solidarity between themselves and other Indians that would emerge from an understanding of a shared history and destiny. The Red-Black people depicted here and others like them represent the best chance for African-Americans and American Indians to be united in celebration.

PHOTOGRAPHS AND NARRATIVES

2 THE RED-BLACK CONNECTION

NELLE BECKER-SLATON, PH.D
Narragansett/Abneki
Providence, Rhode Island
Author, Oral History Instructor, Retired Educator

On my mother's side of the family was from the Narragansett Indian Nation and she identified with that heritage. My great, great grandfather Daniel Perry joined the Revolutionary War with others from the Narragansett Nation. My family went to all of the powwows and often talked about our Indian ancestors. My grandfather on my father's side of the family often discussed his Indian mother of the Abneki tribe from Canada.

My uncle Ernest would always dress up in his Indian regalia and take us to the powwows. My mother, who was a teacher, would often put on summer pageants, both Indian and African American. We had teas once a month at our home, which were attended by African American artists, musicians, and professionals. My mother's second job was writing the society column for the Amsterdam News.

My daughter and I became members of the Daughters of the American Revolution (DAR) due to our patriarch, Daniel Perry, who we documented through family research. We have also done a lot of research on my paternal side and I'm still in touch with cousins on both sides of the family.

I have photographs and an ivory knife brought back from Liberia by my Aunt Ruth who was a missionary nurse and taught in the nursing school there. I also have my Uncle Calvert's Indian pipe.

My friends in Providence, Rhode Island, call me and send news clippings about the Narragansett Indians. My children, and now my grandchildren, go to many Native American events. Recently I donated audiotapes and videotapes on Indians to the downtown Indian center.

When we had family reunions in Rhode Island, we attended a powwow and visited Indian relatives. At a formal dinner, the tribal clerk and elders of the Narraganset nation presented me with an Indian doll in recognition of my ancestor, Daniel Perry, who served on the tribal council. After the ceremony, my >

NELLE BECKER-SLATON, PH.D
Narragansett/Abneki
Providence, Rhode Island
Author, Oral History Instructor, Retired Educator

< children were impressed with a clambake, a custom of the Indians.

   I've also participated in and celebrated my African American culture. I have both Indian and African artifacts in my home. Because of my missionary aunt's influence, we often entertained African students. Two of my three children married Africans.

ASANI CHARLES
Chickasaw/Choctaw
San Francisco, California
Educator

I first became aware of my Indian heritage when I was a young child. I remember watching the TV film, "Roots," and telling my maternal grandmother that one day I would research our family history and go "all the way back to find out who the Africans were." She gave a half smile and responded, "Don't be too surprised when you find more Indians than Africans." My great grandmother, Estella, was half African American and half Chickasaw. Most of the oral history is kept my grandmother who remembers her mother's stories about the Dawes Commission. When she died, her death certificate read "African American/Choctaw." My interest in the family history helped to free her to celebrate her heritage. I continue to do genealogical research to unlock the past so we can know who we truly are.

The first personal experience being openly accepted into the American Indian community without prejudice was at my first pow-wow. An Elder hugged me and that made me feel okay, that I was not a spectator, but would soon be a part of the community. My family recently moved from California to Texas, and here, I'm practically surrounded by Choctaws and Chickasaws. I have learned so much about both my tribes and enjoy the increased opportunity to participate in Stomp Dance, the dance of the Southeastern tribes.

I see things as an African American and as an American Indian and often use the phrase "Red Black" because it's just easier to say. Our cultural experiences have so many parallels that it is no wonder that a good percentage of African Americans have Native roots. My husband and I raise our children within both cultures and they are perhaps the first generation to be able to freely do so without shame of any kind. My five-year old daughter has been dancing in the arena since she was 18-months old. Her older brothers show their cultural pride in their favorite activities, sports and music. I will have failed if my children know less than I do. >

ASANI CHARLES
Chickasaw/Choctaw
San Francisco, California
Educator

< As an educator, I find priceless value in multicultural education and use my classroom to right many of the historic wrongs written in textbooks about Indians. I am constantly challenged to correct the stereotypes my students have of Indians. There are few things more powerful than truth; it changes even the hardest hearts in its own time.

The two cultures I represent cannot be separated; they are in concert in me. I'm the lady at the powwow who pulls out fried chicken and wraps it in fry bread. I think it all boils down to how we are called in life. My mother told me she took a Zulu name and changed the spelling a bit to "Asani," because she liked the meaning of the word. She named me after a South African flower that needs little water to flourish, and interpreted its meaning as "independent." Five years ago, I met a Cree Women's drum group called Asani. I asked them what the name meant in Cree. They told me it means "strength." Independence and strength—these two characteristics go hand in hand. Knowing this, how can I departmentalize who I am? I am as I was brought here. And I celebrate this fact.

DON "LITTLE CLOUD" DAVENPORT
Seminole/Muskogee Creek/Chickasaw (Bird Clan)
Jackson, Michigan
Executive Director, Nonprofit Organization

My great, great grandfather was an African from Sudan. In the early 1800's, he was captured by Arabs, sold into slavery, and taken to the coast of West Africa to be brought to the New World. He escaped from a slave ship and stowed away on a British vessel sailing to the Bahamas where he lived underground in Nassau. In 1818, he immigrated to lower Florida and lived among the Black Musogulges, where he met and fell in love with a woman named Koot of the Muskogee Creek/Chickasaw (Bird Clan). They had sixteen children. I learned from my grandfather that some of his uncles left Florida and went to the Caribbean and Brazil, with one brother working as a doctor and passing as White. His sisters were all married into various tribes.

My grandfather was a medicine person and his spiritual teacher was African as well as Seminole. It was through his teaching that I learned to respect nature and the ways of my people, both Indian and African. I have been taught from birth about Native American and Sudanese cultures by my grandparents and mother. Crafts, language, spirituality, and customs, as well as dance, were everyday occurrences. Stories were told of the early Nubian empire.

I am in possession of a Walking Stick that is inscribed with hieroglyphics. My aunt, who died at the age of 101, handed it down to me for she had chosen me to be the carrier of the family history. The hieroglyphics are based upon my great, great grandfather's historic accounts as well as the story of his passage to this country. Additionally, I have a pair of tribal earrings that are about 300 years old. My elk antler necklace was a gift from a medicine person who instructed me to wear it every day to protect me in my life travels. I've been told that it symbolizes that my ancestors' spirits are with me. Another medicine person, that I did not know personally, left me a beaded sweatshirt decorated with wolves looking up to the sky. His sister told me that its >

DON "LITTLE CLOUD" DAVENPORT
Seminole/Muskogee Creek/Chickasaw (Bird Clan)
Jackson, Michigan
Executive Director, Nonprofit Organization

< purpose and meaning would one day become very clear.

   I participate in powwows, ancestral prayer vigils, sweat ceremonies, rites of passage, pipe ceremonies, corn and ghost dances, Sun dances, and other spiritual ceremonies. I also maintain an ancestral altar and talk with medicine persons. Traditionally, my African religious belief is in some practice of the Islamic faith.

   On my mother's side of the family, most of us honor both cultures. My daughters and granddaughters are being taught as I was, so they can give the same teachings to their children and to the Seventh Generation. Most of my friends are accepting of my dual heritage. Some are intrigued by it. Others are not very knowledgeable about Black Indians. There are some African Americans that think I should only honor the African part of my heritage. When asked about my personal race identity, I simply say that I am biracial, Black and Native American. I choose to honor both cultures for it makes me feel like a whole individual. It is all that I've every known. It is in my blood and is the essence of my life.

Author's Note: Don Davenport is a co-founder of the Black Native American Association

GWEN DAVIS
Mattaponi/Cherokee
Richmond, Virginia
Bookkeeper, Accountant, ANASCA Co-founder

As a person of color, I lived the Black experience in the southeast and remember the "Jim Crow" period and the Civil Rights Movement of the 1960's. My maternal grandmother's sister identified herself as Mattaponi, while my maternal grandfather was descended from slaves. My father identified his father as Cherokee. As a child, it was normal to hear the elders talking about Indian things but I didn't pay it much attention until I was an adult and my mother gave me details about my family heritage.

I hold the drum as dear to both cultures. The first time I was presented to the arena and wore the regalia and danced around the drum was a very important event for me. In celebration of my Indian heritage, I dance, make crafts and share cultural knowledge with people who show interest and respect. I respect our traditions and histories of the Native American people and I have not had negative response to the claim of my heritage, at least not to my face. Many of my friends and associates are Indian and don't make my ethnicity an issue. Strangers generally are curious and want to know more.

I do not have a CDIB (Certificate of Degree of Indian Blood) because it was never an issue when I lived in the southeast. No one in our community was asked to "prove" his or her degree of Indian blood. It was common knowledge that there were lots of Indians living in the "colored" communities and our personal histories were passed down by word of mouth the same as in other Indian families. If I do apply for a CDIB card, I expect to be accepted because I would have the necessary documents. But whether or not I have the documents, I'm still Indian. These papers are subject to legal circumstances but blood speaks no matter what papers say.

As people of color, Indians in Virginia and other parts of the south were subjected to laws of discrimi>

GWEN DAVIS
Mattaponi/Cherokee
Richmond, Virginia
Bookkeeper, Accountant, ANASCA Co-founder

<nation and there was a systematic attempt to erase their Indian identities from the public records.

The "one-drop of Black blood rule" operated in the Indian world much as it did for other "coloreds." Because of this paper genocide, the struggle to maintain their identity pushed some Indians to disassociate themselves from the African American experience and has provoked others to dismiss "Black Indians" in an attempt to maintain their own identities. The government uses games to set elements of the community against one another other and there is fear that the culture is being stolen, sold and perverted. Because of perceived financial advantages to now being Indian, there are real concerns about "mixed bloods" taking over tribal councils without proving their dedication to the culture, and there has been a growing conflict between some full bloods and mixed bloods and between some urban Indians and reservation Indians. There are real concerns in the Indian community

When we make a choice to connect with our heritage, we are making a connection to our past. That connection helps to explain and fill in the holes in our hearts. We must acknowledge our Indian ancestors as well as our Black ancestors—they all deserve to be remembered. That memory should be honored and cherished by carrying on their traditions

PHYLLIS DAVIS
Mattaponi
Richmond, Virginia
Retired Educator

I became interested in soft sculpture doll making while teaching in the Richmond, Virginia Public School System. I realized that this craft sparked an interest in nearly all of the students who were exposed to it. My Indian dolls were especially interesting to the students because, in Virginia, there are many people of Native American and African heritage. Through the use of dolls as teaching aids, I was able to expose students to the different dress and customs of Native Americans from various regions.

SYLVIA DAVIS
Seminole
Shawnee, Oklahoma
Educator

As a Black Seminole Indian, I have a Seminole Freedman number, but have been denied a Certificate of Indian Blood (CDIB) because the Freedmen are classified as former slaves. My grandmother was a full-blooded Seminole Indian and my grandfather was a Black Seminole Indian. My great, great, great, great, great grandfather was William August Bowlegs, a famous chief and leader of the Seminole Nation in the early 1800's. Knowing how important he was in battle against the United States and how close a relationship he had with the Black Indians means a lot to me.

I don't understand why I can't be considered a part of a nation into which my family was born. My grandparents were allotted land in Seminole Indian Country in Oklahoma—160 acres. We have only twenty acres left because the rest was stolen from my family through trickery.

I cherish the pictures I have collected and the stories about Bowlegs and others told over and over to me by tribal members. I attend powwows, eat traditional foods, and attend the Seminole Estilusti funeral celebration ceremony. I sit on the General Tribal Council as a representation of the Black Indian Band.

I have a lawsuit pending against the United States government on behalf of the Black Seminoles to require our enrollment in the nation. People have been very supportive of the legal action and encourage me to continue to fight and not give up.

RENE DEAHL-NAKATA
Creek/Cherokee
Dayton, Ohio
Titleist

My grandmother's family has always claimed its Indian heritage. She was talented in growing and using healing herbs with the knowledge she acquired from her mother and grandmother. I have been able to trace the family history back to the late 1800's, to my great, great, grandmother, Letty. The elders in the family were all born in the heart of Jefferson County, Alabama. My grandmother taught me great respect for nature and its power, how to use it, and to give something back.

I've just recently begun attending powwows to celebrate and honor my grandmother. I find similarities in my Buddhist practice and my "Indianness." Both belief systems have taught me to be still and listen to the forces, to be disciplined. I have tried to teach my children respect for nature, a belief that I hold very dear. Most of my friends are multiethnic and very supportive of my views.

MICHAEL DELUZ
Wampanoag

My heritage includes a great variety of groups. I am a member of the Wampanoag Indian nation, however, my band is not federally recognized and there are no tribal ID's. I'm also Cape-Verdean, Spanish and English. On my father's side in every generation, most of my family identified themselves as Indian. That influence was even stronger than the African American identity.

As kids we were exposed to both Wampanoag and Cape-Verdean cultures from the beginning, with powwows and summer urban celebrations. We attended spiritual ceremonies (sweat lodge and Sundance) and lived for a while in Brazil where the culture is similar to the Cape Verdean, enjoying festive music and delicious food.

STEPHANIE DUPONT
Wampanoag
Pasadena, California
Psychotherapist

My maternal grandmother was Wampanoag, but I grew up with my father and was brought up very middle class—generic American and mainstream. Nevertheless, I have always been drawn to the purity of Native American icons. The information about my family heritage has sparked my curiosity, and I have often wondered what it is about me that reflects my Indian culture. There are also other ethnic strains in my heritage. For example, I have a great grandfather who is Chinese. Despite the reality of my ethnic diversity, sometimes I feel cultureless.

There are many political as well as emotional issues related to claiming one's Indian heritage. I resist an ethnic label because I don't like stereotypes and assumptions. Race doesn't define me. Who we are depends on the context.

ZENOBIA EMBRY-NIMMER
Cherokee
Emporia, Kansas
Community Activist, Writer

My great grandparents walked the Trail of Tears into Arkansas, then to Oklahoma, with other relatives settling in Kansas. As a seventh generation person of mixed culture, I understand the necessity of "standing and representing" my ancestors and my communities of today. At powwows, I participate as a Southern Traditional Dancer. I am very interested in helping others find their true cultural paths and believe it is important to follow the Creator and listen to the ancestors who "whisper in our ears."

As one of the four founders of the Black Native American Association in the San Francisco–Bay Area, I have been deeply involved in the communities I represent, as well as in the community of planet Earth.

I have worked as a community activist for the past 32 years, addressing issues related to social and economic justice in the Bay Area. I have specialized in training businesses about Equal Employment and Housing Opportunity/Civil Rights Law. I am a Wolf Clan person and diligent in carrying out these responsibilities.

ALEANE FITZ-CARTER
Chickasaw
Council Bluffs, Iowa
Educator, Musician

My great grandfather, Spencer Ellis, was a full-blooded Chickasaw Indian and he married my great grandmother who was a slave. The story of how they met and fell in love is a wonderful one that I have written down in short story form. My mother and her sisters were the storytellers in the family and I remember sitting and listening to these accounts of the family history, their stories about the days of slavery and of the days after emancipation.

My maternal grandparents ran away to freedom, while my paternal grandparents were emancipated. My parents migrated to Iowa where I was born. I have old photographs of the family and some of my grandmother's dishes. In addition, I recently acquired Indian artifacts that now grace my home.

My friends and family acknowledge that most Blacks have Indian blood and are very positive about my heritage. I proudly celebrate both my African and Native American heritage by attending powwows, listening to Indian drumming, playing Negro spirituals, and participating in Black History Month and Kwanzaa rituals. Out of these strong cultures come the values I have passed on to my children—endurance, stamina, courage, fairness, tenacity, and most of all, hope.

MICAH FITZ-PATRICK
Blackfeet
San Francisco
Artist, Craftsman

I just say that I am African and First Nations on my father's side and of European descent on my mother's side. I'm claiming all of these heritages whether people like it or not. I don't have a CDIB card at the moment and I would be interested in it only as it furthers my family tree research.

I wanted to learn the story of my parents, their parents, and so on... my story. I wanted to be able to who say I am and be able to break down the Who, What, Why, Where, and When. I talked to the elders on my father's side, like my great Uncle Henry. To the best of his recollection of the family oral history, we had full-blooded ancestors on two branches of the family going back at least three generations. The Blackfeet and Five Tribes are frequently mentioned over the years. God knows who is still waiting to be found.

I sometimes hesitate when asked what tribe I'm claiming. It's not out of shame of having Native roots, though. It's because of the uncertainty of not knowing for sure, at the moment, what tribe. I don't want to come off as a wannabe, trying to cash in on the culture or tribal funds, especially since I don't fit the stereotypical view of what an Indian's supposed to look like. It's the tired, old game of divide and conquer theory and always having to prove ourselves to others, even worse, to each other.

I haven't been able to invest as much time gathering family history, as I would like. It's mostly bits and pieces... like a puzzle. I've written everything down in hopes of one day putting that puzzle together. There are many personal descriptions of our ancestors... how they carried themselves, and how they looked, with comments like "You know, (Grandma, uncle, cousin, etc.) looked like they just stepped off of the Rez". All you have to do is look at the old photos and the family today to see the African/First Nations connection.

As I travel in and out of different cultural circles, I find that the harder people try to separate themselves and focus on the differences, instead of embracing them, the more I discover they're alike. Whether as individuals or a people, they all have a history of oppression and abuse, pain of separation, loss of freedom, land, community, family, language, identity, culture, and respect. Yet there still remains a basic goodness, the ability to love, laugh, sing, dance, and a readiness and willingness to stand and fight for what is right and just. There is a deep reverence for the Creator, even though it's not always evident.

There are a few special things that I like to keep around in the family. For instance, there are two crazy quilts hand sewn by Grandmother Vigor at the age of 67 around 1888. Family surnames are lovingly stitched onto the fabric. I hold dear the honors bestowed on me by my relations and I especially cherish the old family photos. I am an artist so I tend to express myself in that way consciously, and other times subconsciously. Either way, my art usually combines elements of my triple heritage. I'll use traditional material, design, and colors, and I will research each so the art comes out right.

When I mention my heritage, some people react negatively. The negative response occurs anytime I (or people like me) show interest in, read, wear, or listen to something from another part of our heritage other than what they identify with. I guess they think by doing so we are denying that part of ourselves, and ultimately, denying them.

I pass on whatever positive uplifting values I've learned in my short time here—values like honor, responsibility, respect, and pride. I would also like to pass on the skills I've learned as a self-taught artist. I'll share whatever I can with who ever is genuinely interested, especially the wee ones. To not do so would be just plain wrong. Each one teach one, eh?

BILLIE JEAN FRIERSON
Seminole
Del Rio, Texas
Writer, Retired Library Administrator

The heritage of my family is very rich in culture, tradition and love. Our family left a mark of gallantry and courage, from slaves to free men and women to fighters and military heroes. The men and women in my family fought valiantly defending our right to freedom and a place to care for their families, nurture their children and earn a living. Regardless of the inequities in war, my ancestors decided they would rather die fighting for freedom than have their freedom taken away. Jeff Guinn's book, *"Our Land Before we Die: The Proud Story of the Seminole Negro"*, and Kevin Milroy's book, *"Freedom on the Border: the Seminole-Maroons in Florida, the Indian Territory, Coahuila, and Texas"*, are just two of the books that capture the deeds of the Seminole-African American from the arrival of the first ships from Spain to the development of the first colonies to the fight to retain their home in Florida.

Relatives on my father's side include notable Seminole Scouts. My great-great-grandfather, Sergeant John Wood, (along with Pompey Factor and Isaac Payne) received the Congressional Medal of Honor for the heroic rescue of his commander Lieutenant John L. Bullis in 1875. My great-grandfather, Bill Williams, was also a Seminole Scout. His daughter, Gertrude Williams, married Billy Ward, Sr. Gertrude was encouraged to register with the Seminole Nation. At the time, however, she was too sick to complete the process. My Father, Billy Ward Jr., came from this line.

Relatives on my mother's side include my grandparents, John Wilson, and his wife, Nancy Thompson. Nancy was known for her work in the community in Del Rio, Texas. She was so beloved by her peers that the hall of Greater Mount Olive Baptist Church was name in her honor. My mother, Mary Wilson, came from this line. These loved ones no longer walk among us, but they will live in our hearts forever.

I am proud of my heritage and travel annually to the Seminole Program Celebration held on the third week in September in Brackettville, Texas. I love to sit close to the group and listen to the elders recall stories of days gone by, hear the leaders of the Seminole Indian Scout Cemetery Association, and hear the Warrior Band Council share plans for future development and growth. We then feast on traditional dishes of beans, rice, beef, goat, chicken, tortillas, hot-pepper salsa and potato salad. Many are called to participate in the parade and historical program honoring the lives and deeds of our ancestors. No celebration would be complete without culminating in song and prayer on Sunday in honor of our ancestors at the historical site of the Seminole Indian Scout Cemetery.

I was the first African American and Seminole student to receive the Outstanding Woman Student of the Year Award from California State University, Pomona. I wrote the UCLA Law Library Circulation Procedures Manual while at UCLA in the masters program. I went on to serve as librarian and Administsrator for three years in Anaheim and twenty-five years in the Los Angeles County system. I planned and developed multicultural programs that were inclusive. For the first time, Armenia, Hispanic, Samoan, Filipino, Hispanic, and Chinese programs were developed and presented and other ethnic collections were expanded. Throughout my career, I stressed the use of positive images in literature and how to share the multicultural experience in library programs. My brief biography is included in Binnie Tate Wilkin's book, *African American Librarians in the Far West: Pioneers and Trailblazers*.

I have completed research for three children's book: *Seminole Indian Scouts Descendant's Celebration*; *Marian Matthews: California's First African American Librarian*; and *Effie Lee Morris: Leader, Librarian and Coordinator of Children's Services*.

SUSAN GERRARD
Blackfoot/Sioux/Cherokee
Atlanta, Georgia
Retired Nurse

My mother, Big Mom, was Cherokee, Scotch, Irish, and African. Dad was Blackfoot and Sioux. I was the youngest daughter of twenty-one children with Indian bloodlines on both sides of the family. As a child I wore beads, headbands, and braids with bangs. One male member of my family wore his long hair in a bun. The skin coloring in our family ran from white as snow to dark as night.

When I was growing up in Normandy, Missouri, I felt very Indian. The nuns said I had all the characteristics, including a stubborn streak. I can recall when my father took me to a festival and I strayed and got lost. A kindly Indian took my hand and brought me back into the gathering. I felt as though I belonged in that space. I now use the services of the American Indian Health Clinic and feel spiritually uplifted. Often, I feel multiracial and international.

BOE BVSHPO LAWA (MANY KNIVES) GLASSCHILD

Choctaw/Cherokee/Blackfoot
Midland, Texas
Shamanic Healer, ANASCA Co-founder

My Choctaw grandmother raised me in a household that honored both my African and my Choctaw lineage. She was one the original Dawes roll of 1899 and a source of information on the family's history. All her immediate family members were born in Indian Territory, but eventually moved into the cities. Being raised by grandmother made getting a Certificate of Degree of Indian Blood (CDIB) no problem at all.

I can vividly remember how the Choctaws in my family treated each other. I can remember many stories, names, and events, as each year we always returned to Oklahoma for a family gathering. At the gatherings, the elders had a festive time of story telling and joking about their youth. Several of my relatives were medicine people. I would sit for hours as a child listening to their stories of spirit encounters and unusual events that the various family members had experienced. I was always awed by the way my family was with Great Spirit and can vividly remember my initiation into the medicine world on the day of my grandmother's death. A legacy was passed on from her to me to continue through my children, perhaps.

I live in a state of ceremony with the Earth Mother during every walking moment. I hold everything to me that respects my Earth Mother as a sacred being. I strive to see every relationship as a ritual between two events and subscribe to a golden rule of "No harm shall come to Creator's children." I hope to impart to my children the honor of being a medicine person of Black and Red heritage, and also hope that we will continue to rediscover our tribal connections and bring back the sacred ways of our ancestors.

"We do not go forward in life by what we know as much as what we are available to learn."

ARALDO "TONY" GOMEZ
Cherokee
Marchell, Texas
Artist

My mother raised me and she would only say that I was Cherokee, but she never told me details about my heritage. My grandmother lived with us for about three years. She was the first one considered Indian and always said that we were proud people and that I should not forget that. When she died, all of her Cherokee family came from the reservation in Oklahoma.

I hold dear my medicine bag, my way of prayer, and dancing at powwows. At a recent powwow, I was dancing and a stranger presented me with a pair of leggings. He said that he had made them himself, and now knew why, as he offered them to me. I was honored. Some day, I would like to do Sundance. When I pray I like to go to the mountains or the desert. I guess you could call it chanting, and then I pray to the Creator for all the things He has given to use. I have done this ever since I was about eight or nine years old.

I proudly claim both of my heritages, but my father hated my claim to my Indian heritage. My friends accept it, while Blacks, for the most part, don't accept me. My kids are more White than any other race. They are told that they are Black, White, and Indian, but they are Cherokee first.

JEWELLE GOMEZ
Ioway/Wampanoag
Boston, Massachusetts
Writer

My birth papers say I am "colored" and that is how I describe myself. My great grandmother, who was part Black and Ioway, raised me until I was 22 years old. She spoke of her past, what little she could remember, and urged me not to forget that connection. That's how I was able to remember the town Oskaloosa. She'd say it everyday when she combed my hair. She then gave me a handwritten genealogy for her husband who was Wampanoag and a descendant of the Sachem for whom Massachusetts was named. She was proud of that.

My great grandmother's personal anger any time a western came on TV really affected me as a child, as did her cynicism toward Thanksgiving Day. She had a way of being so still sometimes. I always thought of that as her Indian self. When I was a teenager, my grandmother took me to a fair on Cape Cod and I saw Wampanoag people dancing in a circle for the first time and I cried. I wanted so much to be able to dance, too. So I guess stillness and dancing are the two, somewhat contradictory cultural elements, I hold closest to me.

MARY BROUSSARD HARMON
Choctaw/Blackfoot
St. Louis, Missouri
Actress

I've always known that I was part Native American as our family's oral history identified my maternal grandmother as being full-blood Choctaw. When I was in the fifth grade, an Indian Chief came to our school to talk about Indian culture. He picked me out of the crowd to wear the beautiful chief's headdress. He said he could tell I was one of his sisters. I was very proud to be Indian from that moment on.

I didn't really start exploring more of the culture until I was an adult. Now my home includes Native dolls, turquoise jewelry and dream catchers. Sometimes I take the whole family to powwows.

I identify myself as Black/Native American although I am also of European stock. My other family members claim their Indian heritage as well. Sometimes in the Black community you're made to feel that if you're claiming an additional ethnic identity, you think that you're better than someone else. My children have known from the beginning that they were multi-ethnic. I encourage my children to embrace their entire heritage. They will never have to feel like they must choose what race they are.

GENE "QUIETWALKER" HOLMES
Comanche
North Platte, Nebraska
Young Counselor, Administrator, Entertainer, ANASCA Co-founder

I was born on a small reservation in North Platte, Nebraska, and was raised by my maternal great grandmother and great grandfather until I was five years old. This side of the family came from the breakaway of the Shoshone Nation with Quanah Parker, who moved east and then south. My great grandmother explained things to me, talked about the buffalo, and taught me Indian crafts and beading, as well as the language. I took pleasure in the ritual of combing her hair. She gave me the Indian name, "He who walks quiet." My mother changed this to "Quietwalker," which I proudly use to this day. Every two years we have large reunions, which serve to pass on family history, especially our African lineage. There a few remaining members of the Native American side of the family.

When I meditate, I try to remember situations related to my history and family. I use sage and herbs and say Indian prayers. I speak fluent Utoastecian, the language of the Kwahadi band.

My home is full of symbols from both cultures. The symbols I hold closest are the ones passed on to me by my mother and my great grandmother. One in particular is a black leather pouch with tobacco, sage, a stone, and earth from the reservation. It has been a sense of family pride to hand down the culture from both heritages. I have passed on all that I have to my family, taking them to many African/Native powwows and other events. Three rings from my great grandmother are highly valued objects and were handed down to my grandson at his wedding. Other items that I have received from elders will be passed down to my children at some point in their lives.

I also have symbols in my office that are dear to me. In youth counseling services, I use Indian concepts such as the Echo map and I emphasize family support systems. I also encourage youth to explore their African-Indian links. I attend monthly activities such as powwows, and participate in various rituals >

GENE "QUIETWALKER" HOLMES
Comanche
North Platte, Nebraska
Young Counselor, Administrator, Entertainer, ANASCA Co-founder

< and African American events. I play several Native American flutes on a professional level.

There have been people from both communities that react to my heritage on a negative basis and ask, "Who or what are you trying to be?" I have encountered some skeptical comments in the workplace. However, I continue to share my knowledge with other people interested in the African/Native American connection.

ANDREW QUINTEM ISAACS
Cherokee
Kansas City, Kansas
Former Police Officer, Retired Deputy Health Officer

I was raised as Black in a segregated society but I just consider myself an American. My mother's mother was Irish and her father was Black, but my mother would not talk much about her side of the family. My father would tell us about his full-blooded Cherokee grandfather, and had a picture of him with the high cheekbones associated with Indian features. My father was very proud of this heritage.

I enlisted in the army in 1940, just before the beginning of World War II. Units were segregated then, and I served in the 10th Cavalry of the Buffalo Soldiers. There were three other units as well. During that service, all of us had individual horses assigned to us. We were responsible for their training and well-being. Our horses were fed even before we ourselves ate. We learned to break horses, usually wild mustangs from the Plain states, and shoe them.

After World War II, all military forces were integrated and the Buffalo Solider Cavalry units, as such, were disbanded. I was recently elected president of the Los Angeles Chapter of Buffalo Soldiers of the 9th and 10th Horse Cavalry.

Author's note: The original Buffalo Soldiers were used to help settle the West and were, at once Indian fighters, Indian protectors, and had Indian ancestry themselves.

WILMER JAMES
Homa
Los Angeles, California
Artist

My paternal grandmother, a pipe-smoker, was Homa and married to an African. My father died when I was small so I know little about his family. My mother was from Lake Charles, Louisiana and spoke French, but later abandoned the culture. Her father was a French veterinarian, while her mother was Black from Madagascar. Although people on the street often identify me as Indian, I feel I belong to a universal culture.

AVERY MICKEY TRUNELL JOHNSON
Choctaw
Actor

My grandfather was Indian. His mother was Indian and his father Irish. My grandfather and I used to talk a lot when I was little. I learned from him how to plant and grow foods. He taught good survival instincts. He used to say, "I'm not Black. We have a lot of Indian in us." The photograph of his mother, my great grandmother, is my prized possession.

GROVER JOHNSON
Cherokee/Sauk and Fox
Sparkman, Arkansas
Funeral Director

My paternal grandfather was dark with long straight hair and his family was from the West Indies. My father told how his father fled from slave hunters who tried to capture him. Grandpa died when he was 104 years old. My maternal grandmother was part Cherokee and part White. My parents had twelve children and we would travel in large ox-drawn wagons and cook meals in big wash pots. Often other Indians would camp on the family land. Some Blacks will look at me and see me only as a Black man, but lots of people recognize me as Indian.

GEORGIA JOSEPH
Cherokee/Sioux
Memphis, Tennessee
Floral Designer, Community Activist

I grew up in Needles, California, not too far from a reservation and was raised by my paternal grandparents, Will and Flora Wilburn. My siblings and I spent a lot of time at the local river near the home of my aunt and uncle. Older people were always around to tell me stories. As a youth, I always had handmade moccasins, and silver and turquoise jewelry. I enjoyed making and playing with bows and arrows. I was always drawn to the drums. I recall seeing a sacred ceremony—a funeral, I believe—where the drums were played for a week and a woman sang and wailed into the night. My Indian lineage is rooted in both my mother's and father's families. I was encouraged to explore and inquire. I was introduced to my Native American bloodlines when I asked about the Indian man in an old photograph that hung over my grandparents' bed. My papa said, "You see that man? That's your great grandfather."

I did not know my biological father until I met him when I was an adult. It was then that I learned his family had at least one record of Native American blood due to an ancestor from the Yalebushawa Indian tribe in Mississippi.

I burn sage to create sacred space and pray to the four winds. I am also Rastafarian and use incense and candles. I use quiet reflection to center myself as I pursue a spiritual journey. My style of dress and my training as a floral designer bring me closer to nature and express my link to my cultural background. For twenty years, I have been involved in African American studies and have spent years building an understanding of the African America/Native American link, collecting books and meaningful objects. I have only scratched the surface of my Indianness. I share with others the importance of being in touch with spirit, the love of family, tribe collectiveness, and the power of knowing who you are. I strongly feel that African enslavement and the massacre and oppression of the Indians are of equal importance. >

GEORGIA JOSEPH
Cherokee/Sioux
Memphis, Tennessee
Floral Designer, Community Activist

< Foreigners often assume I am from another country. Friends just say I've always been strange or different. Some family members say, "You're trying to be something that you're not!" Others think that that I don't know who I am. One of the proudest days of my life was when African/Native American princesses escorted me into the arena at the African Marketplace Powwow. I felt accepted—at home.

HELEN C. KEY
Blackfoot
Baldwyn, Mississippi
Multi-media Artist, Retired Administration Assistant

Born in 1853, my grandmother was Blackfoot and spoke frequently of the time when Whites enslaved her and her family. She was twelve years old when, at the end of the Civil War, her family moved by covered wagon from southern Mississippi to northern Mississippi. My painting in this photograph is my representation of that journey as described by my grandmother. The painting is called "Freedom." My grandmother had curly black hair that she wore shoulder length in large rolls of curls. Grandma Tilda, as we called her, made hominy and smoked a corncob pipe.

My mother, called Mama, was a talented and good-looking woman. At different times, she was an interior decorator, cook, tailor, and seamstress. She was considered the belle of the town. Mama was a survivor, and one of her favorite expressions was, "I'll not give up; I'll just give out."

KIM LEIGH
Mukwikee, Wisconsin
Los Angeles, California
Affirmative Action Administsrator

My maternal grandmother was a Mukwikee Indian from Ohio and had a child, my mother, from a relationship with a Black man. My mother encountered racial slurs early on. When she traveled through Oklahoma on the train she had to decide which bathroom to use—the one for Whites or the one for Blacks. She later married a Black man who did not allow her to associate with other Indians. After his death, she went back to the Indian community and the American Indian United Methodist Church. She is now totally urban.

I lived with my grandmother for years in Los Angeles. We went to church, powwows, and did arts and crafts. I participated in the Indian club on campus and had Indian friends. I used to think I was Hispanic because my classmates spoke Spanish. My brother is involved on the fringes of Indian culture after having gone through an identity crisis. I have a full-blooded Indian cousin. My mother did not get involved in the culture due to the control of my Black stepfather. She remains uninvolved and may be somewhat jealous of my Indianness.

Although my mother has a tribal number, I don't. There are requirements related to the matrilineal side. Though I identify as Black and am still conflicted about my identity, I can move back and forth between the two cultures. I would like to find ways for Blacks and Indians to work together.

STEPHANIE ROBINSON LINDSEY

Blackfeet/Powhatan/Pamunkey/Mattaponi
Berkeley, California
Distribution Clerk, US Postal Service

I identified with both my Indian and my Black heritage when I was young. Now, I mostly identify with my Native culture. I guess since I'm older now, I feel more comfortable with who and what I am. I'm both, but some attitudes make you want to be just one culture. I can't pick and choose. I'm me—Indian and Black.

Not much from the Black culture was taught in my family. I learned from listening and interacting with other Blacks about Africa, slavery, the arts, dances, and music. There are Indian ancestors on both sides of my family and so the Native culture was expressed a lot through religion, family, healing, art, music and dance. We learned to watch and listen and question. It is very important to cleanse the mind and begin each day with prayer and clarity so one can be open to all that is around you.

My family spoke of living in the hills of Virginia and North Carolina, then moving to Oklahoma before leaving the reservation for jobs. Some passed as mulatto and white, others were considered colored in Virginia. Being Indian and intermarried with Blacks in the 1920's and 1930's brought its own set of problems.

The family continues to explore our roots and have found traces of our European ancestors—Scottish, Irish, Greek, Italian, German, Welsh, English and Dutch—as well as the Native and African.

We are involved in many Native American rituals and traditions such as sweat lodges, burning sage in abalone shells, maintaining medicine pouches for healing stones. My home is filled with Indian items such as a medicine wheel, dream catcher, and burden baskets. We leave small offerings to ancestors, attend powwows, and celebrate Native American History Month.

I've handed down to my children my celebration of Native culture and have taught them to show >

STEPHANIE ROBINSON LINDSEY

Blackfeet/Powhatan/Pamunkey/Mattaponi
Berkeley, California
Distribution Clerk, US Postal Service

< respect for elders, all children of the Almighty, and the animals and beasts of burden. I teach them that you have to be clean of mind and body to dance the powwow trail. Together, we let others know that we are here as Black Indians and are here to stay.

STUART MASON ZAVIER LINDSEY
Blackfeet/Powhatan/Pamunkey/Mattaponi/Chickasaw/Cherokee/Apache
Oakland, California
Student, American Indian Public Charter School

While I am both Black and Native Indian, my mom stresses the Native culture more than my Black-Creole culture. It has been difficult learning to relate to all the diverse cultures that make up my ancestry. Our Native Indian family history goes back to my great, great, great, great grandmother who was a descendent of Pocahontas. I want people to know about Black Indians. We did and do still exist.

My medicine bag, dream catcher, and the blessing with sage are important symbols of indigenous culture. I also attend powwows, Catholic Church, and celebrate customs to honor all of my ancestors.

EDDIE NOBLE MAJET, JR.
Choctaw
Mesa, Arizona
Businessman

I grew up in Mesa, Arizona, a wonderful town of people of all races where everyone got along. I have fond memories of that time and of my mother, Penny Webb. My paternal grandmother was a full-blooded Choctaw from Granada, Mississippi. My paternal grandfather, Bob Majet, was a Navajo chief in Oklahoma. My father was the youngest of twenty-four brothers and three sisters in a close-knit family. On my mother's side, grandfather was Black and my grandmother was Black and Blackfoot. I have always been aware of my two cultures and describe myself as Black and Indian.

When my father was a young boy in Oklahoma in the 1920's, Whites murdered his parents in order to acquire their prime land. It is very serious when a family is killed and others try to assume their culture identity. I'm very concerned when I hear of Anglos who are trying to assume an Indian identity.

The other side of the family has lived in Pasadena, California for over one hundred years. I value my family photographs I have acquired. My greatest passion is reading historical books. I love to read the stories and see photographs that relate to the union of Blacks, Indians, and Mexicans. One of my areas of constant investigation and interest is the failure of schools to teach the full and rich ethnic history of the state of California.

My friends are very supportive of my claim to my heritage. This is especially true of my Indian friends, many of whom also claim their Black heritage. So I am disappointed when Blacks don't claim their Indian blood. I am happy to be one of the spokesmen for unrepresented Indians.

LOUISE MURRAY MIDGET, ED.D
Choctaw
Los Angeles, California
Educator, Playwright, Lyricist

My cultural background is the result of my father's distant, and almost forgotten Yoruba roots, and my mother's more accessible, but often muted, Choctaw Indian heritage. Both my parents were brought up in the Indian Territory in what is now Oklahoma, and the process of their acculturation took place among the mixed Native American and African American population.

Physically, my mother's family closely resembled the Choctaw people. The mixture began before the removal of the Choctaw from Mississippi and continued after their settlement in Oklahoma.

My ancestors walked the Trail of Tears on their way to Indian Territory sometime between 1831 and 1835. Some of there were slaves, and some were slave owners. All of them had access to Choctaw culture, language, and traditions.

Some of the traditions have filtered down to the present-day generations. My mother, grandmother, and great grandmother used herbs for medicinal purposes. I remember drinking sassafras tea, and bitter tasting tansy just because they were good for me. Poke, a leafy vegetable, was added to fresh collards, mustard, and spinach to enhance the flavor of these greens. My mother was very careful not to include the red-purple berries of the poke because they were quite toxic. I remember eating bread-like *banaha* with dinner as well as a variety of grape dumplings that were absolutely delicious.

It was not until I became an adult that I became more intrigued with my Choctaw ancestry. I found a document that increased my curiosity. It was a copy of a land allotment record from the Choctaw Nation giving my mother forty acres of land in Indian Territory. This led me to the genealogy of my mother's family. I have been able to trace my heritage back eight generations and more than 150 years. I have learned that I am a descendant of Amelia Oakes, a Choctaw African American woman. She and >

LOUISE MURRAY MIDGET, ED.D
Choctaw
Los Angeles, California
Educator, Playwright, Lyricist

< her husband, John Oakes, were slaves of Thomas Oakes. Recently I have met and corresponded with the descendants of Thomas Oakes, and we have chosen to experience each other in the present.

    I now actively celebrate my Choctaw heritage with food, music, and dance, regularly attending Choctaw gatherings and intertribal powwows. It has been an incredible journey, and one that is still in progress.

MELANIE MIDGET, D.O.
Choctaw
Los Angeles, California
Physician

My great, great, great grandmother is first identified as Choctaw. Although my grandmother did not freely speak about her Choctaw heritage, she would occasionally let bits of information out. Family photographs and family oral history had led me to understand that my ancestors were not of 100 percent African descent. My genealogical research has lead me straight to the Choctaw Nation by way of documents, including Choctaw slave records. My family has a tribal number that made them quasi-citizens of the nation, but as Freedmen descendants, we do not benefit or enjoy the same rights as other citizens of the Choctaw Nation. We've had difficulty getting information from the nation when they find that we are descendents of Choctaw Freedmen.

I celebrate both my African and Choctaw heritage through food, history, song, language, and cultural celebrations. I've been participating in powwows for a short time and now have Choctaw regalia to wear.

As an African American, I appreciate those who came before me as well as the efforts made and successes experienced in overcoming adversity. As a Choctaw, I appreciate the need to pass on culture, as undiluted as possible, to those who come after me.

Family and friends have been supportive as well as interested in my claim to my Choctaw heritage. I don't have problems with Caucasian strangers when I explain my ancestry. I've found that African Americans tend to question me more, as well as doubt my claims and motives. They need to learn that there are African Americans who celebrate many aspects of their different heritages. There is not a monolithic African American culture that overshadows or envelops other heritages.

ROBERT MILLER, SR.
Cherokee
Minneapolis, Minnesota
Director of Center for Youth at Risk

I am a human being and what you see is what you get. I simply am what I am. My family's oral history goes back to 1811 and includes a great, great grandparent who was Cherokee. Our family has strong bonds and we hold a yearly gathering. I have a collection of weapons of war and of pipes of peace, which I consider very important.

MICHELLE NICHOLS
Choctaw/Cherokee
Mountain View, California
Physician

I am a blend of my father's Black and Native American lineage and my mother's European Ancestry. I consider myself a blend of these three distinct heritages. The development of my appreciation for diversity in individuals, attitudes, and beliefs is the result of growing up multiracial in a family that valued all my ethnicities. While I was growing up, society and certain ethnic groups encouraged a separation of ethnic identity. I felt pressured to affiliate with only one group. A major part of my childhood and adolescence involved carving out a niche for myself, developing a positive identity connected with all three side of my heritage.

The majority of my family history has been passed down orally and only recently has information been uncovered. My sister, Valerie, is compiling documentation and has been successful in piecing together many important pieces of our history.

While at UC Davis, I stayed closely connected to the Native American Community. One of my most enjoyable experiences was teaching science courses at DQ University, a Native American junior college. While my primary focus during medical school at UC San Francisco was on patient care, it was important to me to continue service my community. I was actively involved with Native American Health Alliance and was an executive board member of the Association Students. I worked to provide solutions to health care issues affecting minorities and underserved populations in the San Francisco-Bay Area. Much of my clinical experience was focused on them. I envision a career for myself in internal medicine. I want to provide compassionate care and I'm committed to patient advocacy for people from all communities and backgrounds.

VALERIE NICHOLS
Choctaw/Cherokee
Mountain View, California
Educator

When asked what my ethnicity is, I usually reply, "I was here, I came here, and I was brought here." So I identify as Native American, White, and Black. Sometimes members of the Black community will tell me I am too light-skinned or they will tell me I have to choose only one ethnic identification.

As I am multiracial, my parents have always believed that I ought to know about all parts of my heritage. They always made me feel proud of my diversity. While at UCLA, I participated in the American Indian Student Association (AISA).

The majority of my family history is oral. I have researched for documentation but it has been very difficult to find. For many years, no one would talk about what they knew. Now information is pouring forth. In fact, my aunt has written a book compiling both oral history and documentation.

My daughter and I enjoy making fry bread together. We both wear beaded hair ornaments, mine being ones I received as a child. We attend powwows together and I spend a lot of time dispelling stereotypes and reading to her culturally current books such as, *Black is Brown is Tan*, *Nappy Hair*, and *Coyote Stories for Children*.

I give presentations to my daughter's class, as well as to classes at my school. The lessons are on culture and are to inform kids that Indians are not historic characters, but are living, breathing people who are in their own communities. I take the opportunity during Columbus Day and Thanksgiving celebrations to teach my students the true historic significance of those days.

KAREN SUTTON
Wicomico/Cherokee
Baltimore, Maryland
Historical Interpreter, Professional Genealogist

I describe myself as African American because that is what I physically appear to be and this is the culture in which I was raised and with which I identify, even though I also have White and Indian blood.

The Wicomico lived in the northern neck of Virginia during pre-contact and colonial times. One of my maternal ancestors, John Pinn, served in the American Revolution. When he wrote for his pension, John said he was from Indian Town, Lancaster County, Pennsylvania, and that one parent was a "mustee" and the other Cherokee. My paternal grandfather, Berkley Mack Sutton, Sr., had Indian features and was said to be Cherokee. One of my maternal great aunts was said to be Indian although no one seems to know which nation. I wrote my master's thesis on my free Black ancestors who also happed to be part Native American and part White.

For each baby shower in the family, I put together a customized baby book telling the story of our ancestors and include a pedigree chart that is as complete as possible linking the child to ancestors. For weddings, I do a framed wall chart with the story as an accompanying booklet.

Most of the family and friends and people I meet are fascinated by my heritage. Some want to know more. Others want to know how I know, and how they can find out about their family history and backgrounds. And most Black folks like to brag on their Indians. I tell people, "No one in America is 100 percent anything unless you just got off the space ship. Massa was in your slave quarters, too."

CATHI CAMILLE TERRY-HUGHES
Chickasaw/Choctaw
Oklahoma City, Oklahoma
Social Service Worker

When I was very young, outsiders would ask me about my ethnic background. I consider myself both native African and Native American. My great, great, great grandfather was Indian. My great grandmother gave me a bracelet that had been given to her by her Indian aunt. My elders told me about our history and customs and my cousins and I exchange a lot of information about the family. I treasure hearing words from another language other than English and hearing the stories.

Some of the activities I engage in to celebrate Indian culture include the preparation of corn pudding, hot water corn bread and brewing teas to help in case of illnesses. I attend some powwows and tell my stories to young people.

JOHN RED THUNDER
Choctaw/Blackfoot
Los Angeles, California
Singer, Dancer

I grew up in South-Central Los Angeles and in the Black experience. I always knew I was Choctaw but just never really thought about it. My great grandmother was Choctaw and said we have to be who we are. I came to a fuller Indian understanding when I was about twenty-five years old and living in Hollywood. It was a time for me to reflect on my identity. After several youthful experiences, I came to a moment of clarity. Choctaw blood gave me the link with a long history, with the land, and a way of being with it.

How does that help me in a practical sense? What is the relevance to daily life? What is the validity of the Indian myth as Earth's caretakers? I've always had a concern for the land and have learned that we need to relate to where we are. We need to move through various states of identity with the earth. We need to develop ways of looking at the earth and life interests. We need to develop a respect for the spirit of all creatures, both organic and inorganic. We need to seek ways of living lightly on the land and peacefully. We must make a strong effort to leave the best in place for the next seven generations.

I'm basically Choctaw and I pray in Choctaw. Being Choctaw takes precedence when I'm in that context. I am working on getting things done for my people in non-intrusive ways, especially through the use of ceremony. Although my family doesn't fully understand my involvement with my Indian heritage, they accept it.

STELLA J. VAUGH
Cherokee/Choctaw
Retired Nurse

When I was growing up, I was unable to say I'm Native American, White, and/or Black. I don't have to hint any more. In fact, I'm having fun boasting about my mixed heritage. I jokingly say I'm Heinz 57 variety. Among other ethnic strains, my mother's mother is Cherokee and Irish. My father's mother is Bohemian and his father, Choctaw. I am told that one of my ancestors is of the Black race, and I'm still searching for that beautiful person.

I'm proud of what I am. And I pray that some day the Great Spirit allows me to walk in the beauty of Mother Earth and the rainbow always touches my shoulder. You see, we are all the same in His eyes.

ANGELA Y. WALTON-RAJI
Choctaw Descendant/Choctaw Freedman Descendant
Fort Smith, Arkansas
University Administrator

I am an African American of Choctaw descent. I was born on the border of the Choctaw Nation and was raised to be aware that Choctaw history and culture were part of my family legacy. I grew up in the African American community during the height of the Civil Rights movement. Summers were often spent visiting relatives in nearby Oklahoma.

Sally Walton, my great grandmother, was born in the Choctaw Nation in 1863 and died at the age of ninety-eight. She was the matriarch of our family. Her mother, Amanda, was half Choctaw and half Black. Amanda's parents were James, a Choctaw, and Kitty, a slave. Sally lived with my grandmother where she practiced many aspects of culture, speaking Choctaw with her brother, Joe, when he visited. From Sally pulling herbs to speaking Choctaw to making sassafras tea for me—it was just a part of the life that I knew.

I have family documents I treasure, including artifacts that pertain to Sally's land in the Choctaw nation. I also have the family Bible with birth and death entries of ancestors from Indian Territory. There is interesting oral family history, but our ties to Choctaw history and culture came through Sally. She was our living connection to the Chahta and Chahta Lusa (Choctaw and Black Choctaw). My energies are spent in capturing some of the stories of those elders who were the children of the Freedmen from the various Indian nations. I work to preserve this unique history and am currently directing a Choctaw-Chickasaws Freedman Oral History project. I also publish the Chata-Chickasaw Lusa, a newsletter devoted to the education of the readership about the culture of our ancestors.

I live within an African American cultural context and approach the world from that perspective. My self-knowledge comes from the history that I heard of our ties to the Choctaw Nation as well as the >

ANGELA Y. WALTON-RAJI
Choctaw Descendant/Choctaw Freedman Descendant
Fort Smith, Arkansas
University Administrator

< Black community. I still go to Oklahoma every summer and visit the cultural sites and burial grounds, documenting those of the Black Choctaw.

Many people are fascinated by the history, disappointed when they hear of the estrangement of the two peoples from each other, and devastated emotionally to learn of the Black chattel slavery practice by the Five nations of Oklahoma. These truths go against their perception of an unbreakable alliance between Red and Black people. Younger people that I meet are the most surprised because this is history not taught in Oklahoma schools. The older generation is less shocked, for they lived in the years after statehood and experienced the gradual disenfranchisement of the Freedman and their descendants from the nations.

In most societies, women are the culture bearers and the influence of my female ancestors continues to this day. From my mother comes a rich African American legacy ranging from literature to music. From my grandmother comes the strong interest in providing something that lasts and gives warmth. I attribute my quilt making to her. And from my dear great grandmother comes the Chata culture that influences my interest in cultivating life from the soil. I share these traditions with my niece and my goddaughter. Most importantly, I learned from my mother an appreciation of the past. It was her stories about our ancestors that began my quest to document my entire past—both African and Native American. Both groups inform what I do. I get great satisfaction from them—*Achukma hoke*—it is all good.

ELNORA TENA WEBB-MITCHELL, PH.D
Cherokee/Blackfoot/Choctaw
Los Angeles, California

I considered myself to be a Black Native American of multi-ethnic origin. I have ancestry from France, Spain, and India as well. I became aware of my Native American heritage through my childhood experiences with one of my foster mothers, who as also Black Native American. She never spoke about who she was. Instead, she honored her ancestry through the many practices including rearing of animals, growing plants for nutritional and healing purposes, makings clothes, the display of family photographs on the wall, and through private prayers.

My grandparents and other members of my family were identified as Native American. However, there is much information about our ancestry that is kept secret. Many family members did not revere or honor Indian ancestry. The primary gatekeeper, my aunt, is not open to discussing specifics about the family. Indeed, she has thwarted my efforts to discuss the history with other family members. Most of the family show a disinterest, and a few are embarrassed. Only one brother seems to respect and admire my decision to embrace my Native American heritage. Some friends are supportive and a few expressed discomfort both directly and indirectly. However, it is more important that I live with integrity and experience being my highest self.

My multiethnic origins are acknowledged with symbols and practices:
- African heritage—the Ankh that I incorporated in my Indian regalia, because it symbolizes eternal life
- Blackfoot heritage—the intuitive ability to know, to remember
- Cherokee heritage—the diamond because it symbolizes the four corners of life—the North, South, East, and West—each providing us with safety, nutrition, direction, and hope

THE RED-BLACK CONNECTION

ELNORA TENA WEBB-MITCHELL, PH.D

Cherokee/Blackfoot/Choctaw
Los Angeles, California

- French heritage: the reserved nature that exercises caution so as to render one safe, even when walking into a dangerous den
- East Indian heritage—understanding the importance of tasty, attractive and welcoming food that nourishes the body, mind, and spirit
- Spanish heritage—the desire for life as demonstrated through my walk, talk, laughter, singing, and overall style of movement

I express, celebrate and participate in each culture by acknowledging the presence of my ancestors daily, being conscious in all moments with others, all life forms, mediating, praying and giving thanks to the Great Spirit for allowing me and all aspects of me—other people, the trees, animals, plants, soil, butterflies, water, wind, sky—to be in order for the Source Unconditional Love, the experience being outside of its true nature.

The way I am is the same way I impart these cultural ideals and rituals to friends and others around me. I'm part of community prayer vigils. During these gatherings, altars are built using traditional herbs, plants and instruments. All the things I have access to are blessed and thanked for their support of my life through their presence.

NICHOLAS "LITTLE FEATHER" YOUNG

Cherokee/Creek/Choctaw/Osage
Berkeley, California
Student

My father and other family elders made me aware of my multi-ethnic heritage. My Indian blood comes from both sides of my family and dates back to before the "Trail of Tears." I enjoy going to ceremonies with my dad, and spending time in nature. My heritage is very important to me.

ROBERT "WAYA" YOUNG
Cherokee/Creek/Choctaw/Osage
Berkeley, California
Teacher, Musician

I became aware of my dual heritage through the teachings of my parents and other family elders. My Indian heritage goes back five generations on both my mother's side and my father's side. My mother's heritage has been traced back to 1756.

My sacred pipe and my feathers are cherished possessions. I participate in pipe ceremonies, vision quests, powwows, and sweat ceremonies while fighting for the rights of my people. The importance of ceremony and giving respect to Mother Earth and all my relations are values that I shared with other family members.

ADDITIONAL PHOTOGRAPHS

BELINDA ADAMS
Cherokee

K.C. CLARKE
Blackfoot

ZAIRE DUPONT
Wampanoag

MICHAEL FINCHAM
Seminole

VERDAWN FINCHAM
Seminole

HILLERY GLASSCHILD
Cherokee

  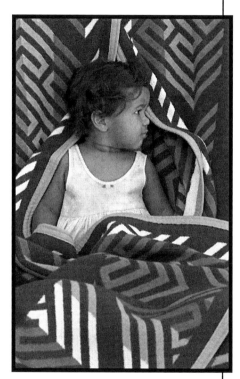

SHANNON GOMEZ
Choctaw/Cherokee/Blackfoot

SHYLO GOMEZ
Cherokee

BROOKE HARMON
Choctaw/Blackfoot

MAYA HARMON
Choctaw/Blackfoot

ROSALYN HOWARD
Sioux

JERRY MCCROY
Cherokee

MAGGIE MCGEE
Choctaw

EDGAR MOLETTE
Choctaw

ANGELA MOLETTE
Choctaw

AFTERWORD

Even as African-Native Americans, the degree to which we claim our culture varies; the elements that we emphasize vary. Bring into the picture the fact that many of us have European, and sometimes, Asian ancestry as well, the reality of who we are becomes even more complex. In the human experience, race, ethnicity, history, culture, training, experiences, beliefs, attitudes, needs, and desires are all part of a swirling wind of influences that shape us and create our uniqueness. The survival of human kind as a species does not depend upon our all becoming identical, but upon our ability to recognize and value this individual uniqueness. We can recognize, acknowledge, and celebrate all of who we are in our journey to become all that we can become.

APPENDIXES

A. BIBLIOGRAPHY

Debo, Angie. *The Rise and Fall of the Choctaw Republic.* Norman: University of Oklahoma Press, 1972.

Forbes, Jack. *Black Africans and Native Americans: Color, Race, and Caste in the Evolution of Red-Black Peoples.* Urbana: University of Illinois Press, 1993.

Franklin, John Hope, *From Slavery to Freedom: A History of Negro Americans.* New York, McGraw Hill, 1994.

Hooks, Bell. *Black Looks: Race and Representation.* Boston: South End Press, 1992.

Hughes, Langston, Milton Meltzer, and C. Eric Lincoln. *Four Centuries of Black Life: African American History.* Scholastic Trade, 1983.

Katz, William Loren. *Black Indians: A Hidden Heritage.* New York: Atheneum, 1986.

Katz, William Loren. *Black Women of the Old West.* New York: Atheneum, 1995.

Katz, William Loren. *Proudly Red and Black: Stories of African and Native Americans.* New York: Atheneum, 1995.

Lindenmeyer, Otto. *Black History: Lost, Stolen or Strayed.* Avon, 1970.

Root, Maria, editor. *Racially Mixed People in America.* Newbury Park: Sage Publications, 1992.

Taylor, Quintard, *In Search of the Racial Frontier.* New York: Norton, 1998.

Weatherford, Jack. *Native Roots: How the Indians Enriched America.* New York: Crown, 1991.

Wright Jr., J. Leitch. *The Only Land They Knew.* New York: The Free Press, 1981.

B. RELATED RESOURCES
Books

_____. *Blacks in the Westward Movement*. Washington: Smithsonian Institution Press, 1975

Abel, Annie Heloise. *The American Indian as Slaveholder and Secessionist: A Chapter in the Diplomatic History of the Southern Confederacy*. Cleveland: Arthur Clark Co., 1915.

Baker, I. and J. Baker. *The WPA Oklahoma Slave Narratives*. Norman: University of Oklahoma Press, 1966.

Belous, Russel, editor. *America's Black Heritage*. Los Angeles, 1969.

Bier, Lisa. *American Indian and African American People, Communities and Interactions: Annotated Bibliography*. Westport: Praeger Publishers, 2004.

Blu, Karen. *The Lumbee Problems: The Making of an American Indian People*. 1980.

Bontemps, Alex. *Black Comanche Boy*. New York: Hill and Wang, 1970.

Bragi, David Arv. *Invisible Indians: Mixed-Blood Native Americans Who Are Not Enrolled in Federally Recognized Tribes*. Tucson: Grail Media, 2006.

Brennan, Jonathan, editor. *When Br'er Rabbit Meets Coyote: African-Native Literature*. Urbana: University of Illinois, 2003.

Britten, Thomas. *A Brief History of the Seminole-Negro Indian Scouts*. New York: Mellen Press, 1999.

Brooks, James, editor. *Confounding the Color Line: The Indian-Black Experience in North America*. Lincoln: University of Nebraska Press, 2002.

Brown, Cloyed. *Black Warrior Chiefs: A History of the Seminole Negro Indian Scouts: A True Story*. Fort Worth: C. I. Brown, 1999.

Brown, Dorothy. *Black Warrior Chiefs: A History of the Seminole Negro Indian: A True Story*. Forth Worth: C.I. Brown, 1999.

Brown, Virginia Pounds, editor. *Creek Indian History*. University of Alabama Press, 1999.

Carpenter, Cecelia. *How to Research American Indian Blood Lines*. Orting: Heritage Quest, 1987.

Debo, Angie. *A History of the Indians of the United States*. Norman: Oklahoma University Press, 1970.

Debo, Angie. *The Rise and Fall of the Choctaw Republic*. Norman: Oklahoma University Press.

Debo, Angie. *The Road to Disappearance*. Norman: University of Oklahoma Press, 1967.

Dinnerstein, Leonard, Roger Nichols, and David Reimers. *Natives and Strangers: Blacks, Indians, and Immigrants in America*. New York: Oxford University Press, 1979.

Dramer, Kim. *Indians of North America: Native Americans and Black Americans*. Philadelphia: Chelsea House, 1997.

Durham, Philip and Everett Jones. *The Adventures of the Negro Cowboys*. New York: Dodd, Mead, 1969.

Ehle, John. *Trail of Tears: The Rise and Fall of the Cherokee Nation*. New York: Double Day, 1988

Flickinger, Robert Elliot. *The Choctaw Freedmen and the Story of Oak Hill Industrial Academy*. Fonda, Journal and Times Press, 1914.

Fogelson , Raymond D. *Handbook of National American Indians, Volume 14: Southeast*. Washington D.C.: Smithsonian Books, 2004.

Gibson, Arrell. *The Chickasaws*. Norman: University of Oklahoma, 1971.

Green, Lorenzo. *The Negro in Colonial New England*. New York: 1968

Guinn, Jeff. *Our Land Before We Die: The Proud Story of the Seminole Negro*. New York: Tarcher/Putnam, 2002

Halliburton, Jr., R. *Red Over Black: Slavery Among the Cherokee Indians*. Westport: Greenwood Press, 1976.

Hampton Normal and Agricultural Institute, *The Hampton Normal and Agricultural Institute and its Work for Negro and Indian Youth*, 1899. Hampton: Institute Press, 1899.

Harris, Julia. *The Black-Indian Connection in American Art*. Hampton: Hampton University Museum, 2000.

Hoover, Dwight. *The Red and The Black*. Chicago: Rand McNally, 1976.

Howard, Rosalyn. *Black Seminoles in the Bahamas*. Gainesville: University Press of Florida, 2002.

Johnson, Kenneth, Jonathan Leader and Robert Wilson, editors. *Indians, Colonists, and Slaves: Essays in Memory of Charles H. Fairbanks*. Gainesville: University of Florida, 1985.

Katz, William Loren. *The Black West*. New York: Simon and Schuster, 1976 1987.

Katz, William Loren. *Proudly Red and Black: Stories of African and Native Americans*. New York, Atheneum, 1993

Lauber, Almon Wheeler. *Indian Slavery in Colonial Times with the Present Limits of the United States*. Williamstown: Conner House, 1970.

Leckie, William. *The Buffalo Soldiers*. Norman: Oklahoma University Press, 1967.

Lindsey, Donald. *Indians at Hampton Institute, 1887-1923*. Urbana: University of Illinois Press, 1995.

Littlefield, Jr., Daniel. *Africans and Creeks: From the Colonial Period to the Civil War*. Westport: Greenwood Press, 1979.

Littlefield, Jr., Daniel. *Africans and Seminoles: From Removal to Emancipation*. Westport: Greenwood Press, 1977.

Littlefield, Jr., Daniel, *The Cherokee Freedmen: From Emancipation to American Citizenship*, Westport: Greenwood Press, 1978.

Littlefield, Jr., Daniel. *The Chickasaw Freedmen: A People Without a Country*. Westport: Greenwood Press, 1980.

Littlefield, Jr., Daniel. *Seminole Burning: A Story of Racial Vengeance*. University Press of Mississippi, 1996.

Marks, Paula Mitchell. *In a Barren Land: The American Indian Quest for Cultural Survival*. New York: Willam Morrow, 1988.

Monceaux, Morgan, and Ruth Datcher. *My Heroes, My People: African Americans and Native Americans in the West*. New York: Frances Foster Books, 1999.

May, Katja. *African Americans and Native Americans in the Creek and Cherokee Nations, 1830-1920's*. New York: Garland, 1996.

Malcomson, Scott L. *One Drop of Blood: The American Misadventure of Race*. New York: Farrar, Straus and Giroux, 2000.

McReynolds, Edwin. *The Seminoles*. Norman: University of Oklahoma, 1957.

Mulroy, Kevin. *Freedom and the Border: The Seminole Maroons in Florida, the Indian Territory, Coachuila, and Texas*. Lubbock: Texas Tech University Press, 1993.

Nash, Gary. *Red, White, and Black: The Peoples of Early America*. Englewood Cliffs: Prentice-Hall, 1974.

Olson, James and Raymond Wilson. *Native Americans in the Twentieth Century*. Urbana: University of Illinois Press, 1984.

Opala, Joseph. *A Brief History of the Seminole Freedmen*, Austin, 1980.

Parry, Ellwood. *The Image of the Indian and the Black Man in American Arts, 1590-1900*. G. Braziller, 1974.

Perdue, Theda. *Slavery and the Evolution of Cherokee Society, 1540-1866*. Knoxville: University of Tennessee Press, 1979.

Peters, Virginia Bergman. *The Florida Wars*. 1979.

Porter Kenneth, Alcione Amos, and Thomas Senter. *The Black Seminoles: History of a Freedom-Seeking People*. Gainesville: University of Florida Press, 1996.

Porter, Kenneth Wiggens. *The Negro on the American Frontier*. New York: Amo Press, 1971.

Sider. Lumbee. *Indian Histories: Race, Ethnicity, and Indian Identity in the Southern United States*. 1993.

Silver, Timothy. *A New Face on the Countryside: Indians, Colonists, and Slaves in South Atlantic Forest, 1500-1800*. 1990.

Smith, Michael. *Mardi Gras Indians*. 1994.

Staton, Max. *The Not So Solid South*. 1971.

Usner, Daniel, Jr. Indians, *Settlers and Slaves in a Frontier Exchange Economy: The Lower Mississippi Valley before 1783*. Williamsburg: University of North Carolina, 1992.

Van Sertima, Ivan. *They Came before Columbus: The African Presence in Ancient America*. New York: Random House, 1977.

Viola, Herman. *After Columbus: the Smithsonian Chronicle of the North American Indians*. Washington D.C.: Smithsonian Books, 1990.

Walton, George. *Fearless and Free: The Seminole Indian War, 1835-1842*. Indianapolis, Bobbs-Merrill, 1997.

Walton-Raji, Angela. *Black Indian Genealogy Research: African American Ancestors Among the Five Civilized Tribes*. Bowie: Heritage Books, 1993.

Winterhawk, Nomad. *Circular Thought: An African-Native American Traditional Understanding*. Santa Ana: Quiet Warrior Publishing, 2005.

Woodford, Dee Parmer. *Finding a Place Called Home: A Guide to African American Genealogy and Historical Identity, 1999.*

Wright, Jr., Leitch. *Creeks and Seminoles: The Destruction and Regeneration of the Musogulge People.* Lincoln: University of Nebraska Press, 1986.

Films

Black Indians: An American Story. Dallas: Rich-Heape Films, Inc., 2000.

How to Trace Your Native American Heritage. Dallas: Rich-Heape Films, Inc., 1998.

The Trail of Tears: Cherokee Legacy. Dallas: Rich-Heape Films, Inc., 2005

Journals and Magazines

American History Illustrated

American Indian Quarterly

American Quarterly

The Black Experience in America: Selected Essays

Colonial Latin American Historical Review

Cultural Survival

Ethnic and Racial Studies

Ethnohistory

Explorations in Ethnic Studies

Florida Historical Quarterly

South Carolina Historical Magazine

Freedomways

Journal of American History

Journal or Ethnic Studies

Journal of Negro History

Journal of Southern History

Louisiana History

Monthly Review

Panhandle-Plains Historical Review

Phylon

Red River Valley Historical Review

Southwestern Historical Quarterly

Websites

Websites are an important source for information and the exchange of ideas. You can also search using keywords such as Black Indians, Freedmen, or the name of the specific Indian nation.

African Native American History and Genealogy Web Page	Black Native American Association
The African-Native Genealogy Website	Culture and Lifestyle of the Estelusti
Black Indians Want a Place in History	Daniel Littlefield
Black African American Natives	Nzinga's Nation-Black Indians
Black Indians: An American Legacy	Slavery in the Cherokee Nation
Black Indians: An American Story	The Estelusti
Black Indian Slave Narratives	Weyanoke

C. HISTORIC OVERVIEW

The lives of Africans and American Indians have been intricately intertwined for at least five hundred years. Even prior to the landfall of Columbus, there is evidence of the African presence in the Americas as documented by Ivan Van Sertima, *"They Came Before Columbus."* The relationship between these two peoples has been one of rescue, mutual assistance, and sometimes, abuse and strife.

At the time of Columbus, there were an estimated eighty million Indians in the Western Hemisphere. Columbus, along with the Spanish and Portuguese, kidnapped a total of almost sixty thousand Indians during their voyages. These enslaved Indians were dispersed throughout Europe as laborers, domestics, and miners. Most of the Indians in the mines died by the age of twenty-six. It was this high death rate that prompted Spanish slave traders to petition their government for an increase in African slavery.

The first Spanish slave traders landed in 1502 on the southeastern coast of what is now Florida. As would often happen, some slaves jumped ship and fled to the woods and the protection of local Indians. Indians and Africans learned they had a common foe, the Europeans. Indians realized that Africans knew European strategies and could provide information helpful to the Indians. Africans often served as translators between the European and Indian populations. Africans realized that Indians knew the land and how to survive on it. In addition, Indians and Africans shared sensibilities based upon common beliefs such as reverence for nature, life, family, religion, economic cooperation, and ancestors. While there were some differences between the two groups, they also shared negative experiences. They suffered from the burdens of slavery, oppression, loss of land, and erosion of traditions and customs.

The British began colonization of the United States in 1619 with the establishment of Jamestown. Among the population were African and European indentured servants who worked off their ocean passage for twelve years. There was ample opportunity for contact between Africans, Indians, as well as Europeans, in the colonies. Over time, and despite class, culture, color, and custom, the proximity of Africans and Indians resulted in the development of Red-Black people. The evolution of the American Black in the South is due in great part to the cultural and genetic contributions of Indians. African-Indian unions were found on Indian reservations and living among the colonies, especially along the eastern seaboard. By the mid-1600's, there were 100,000 African-Indian unions, some with White blood.

When the British began the enslavement of Indians and Africans, the plantations and slave quarters presented the best opportunity for the continued mingling of these two groups. Of course, many slaves would flee the plantations and seek refuge with neighboring friendly Indian tribes. As a result, the British introduced their model of slavery to these Indians. By the mid-

1770's, slavery and its attitudes were entrenched in the cultures of the Five Civilized Tribes—the Choctaw, Creeks, Chickasaw, Cherokee, and the Seminoles. Race and color became important in judging people.

In 1807, the English outlawed the Atlantic slave trade and slavery was confined to Africans, African Americans, and those Red-Black people already enslaved, a total of one million people. By the beginning of the 1800's, Indians east of the Mississippi had become a biracial people with a sprinkling of White blood. Laws were enacted in an attempt to restrict these mixed marriages. Mixed Indian groups were declared no longer Indian and Thomas Jefferson took federal recognition away from several tribes. By mid-century, there were four million African and Red-Black slaves.

President Andrew Jackson's expansionist policies lead to the Indian Removal Act of 1830 and called for the mass deportation of Indians, those same Five Civilized Tribes. Six thousand Indians and their slaves were relocated into Indian Territory, many dying along the trail. Despite the drastic results of removal from their homelands, the tribes continued slavery as a major part of life, and for most part, supported the Confederacy during the Civil War. The tribes, after fighting on the losing side of the war, were required to adopt their freed slaves, many of whom were blood kin. These Freedmen were to be free and equal within the tribe. The reality was that Black members of the nations faced years of legal challenges and mounted political protests in attempt to win citizenship rights, land, education, and equality of opportunity.

In 1907, the former Indian Territory was admitted to the union as Oklahoma and segregation was implemented with Jim Crow Laws that discriminated against Blacks. Indians finally gained United States citizenship in 1924 and disassociated themselves from Blackness based upon the racial caste system in the United Sates. Indians with African ancestry had a special reason to insist they were Indians, not Negroes.

Thus a breach developed between the those people seen as Indians and those who had African ancestry. Along with Jim Crow laws and the withdrawal of federal recognition, two additional factors greatly affected ties between Indians and Blacks. One factor was the Indian relocation into reservations. The second was the mass migration of Blacks from the rural south to the industrial northern cities in the 1940's. These factors have made it hard for the two groups to recover from their alienation and to assert their mutual bond.

In today's world, those with Indian and African ancestry aren't always well received. There is often a stigma associated with an African-American claiming Indian blood. Whites and other Indians might call them "wannabees," especially if they don't look Indian. They might be accused of deserting the race by other African-Americans.

Today, many Indian nations are going through the tedious and costly process of regaining lost federal recognition. They are very cautious about acknowledging mixed heritage due to the fear of having their application for recognition rejected. Freedmen of the Five Civilized Tribes in Oklahoma still face problems gaining access to records to trace their family trees and are are being thwarted by changes in policies of tribal membership. The advent of tribal casinos has created additional tension that often has racial overtones. The problems of Indian identity with its mixedblood/fullblood and color/quantum connotations stem from attitudes and ideas fostered by White culture and destructive government policies over hundreds of years.

The results of the 2000 United States census and its new categories for collecting information about race and ethnicity were very revealing. Two million people identified as American Indian while another two million checked off American Indian along with a second ethnic category. Fully ten percent of the thirty-three million African-Americans checked off two or more ethnic/racial categories, including that of American Indian. The success of biracial Indians such as Lillian Cepa (Ms Indian World of 2000) and popular musicians, the Neville Brothers. have stimulated conversation. Their success and the new identity options will make it easier for African-Americans to claim and celebrate their Indian birthright, and for Indians to claim their long-denied African heritage.

D. HISTORIC RED-BLACK PEOPLE
Selected List

Cripus Attucks: 1723-1770; Natick Indian and Black; first patriot to die in the struggle during the American Revolution.

Josephine Baker: 1906-1975; descendant of Apalachee Indians and Black slaves of South Carolina; dancer, singer, actress, and civil right activist; rose to fame in France, winning the Legion of Honor.

Paul Cuffee: 1759-1817; father was from Ghana and his mother was Wampanoag; entrepreneur and mariner; richest man of color in United States at the time; married a Wampanoag and built a school for African Quakers; thought of himself as Red-Black early on but later became interested in African colonization.

Jimi Hendrix: 1947-1971; music icon; had Cherokee ancestry and was out spoken about the plight of American Indians; two of his songs were inspired by his Indian heritage; first musician inducted into Native American Music Awards Hall of Fame.

Langston Hughes: 1902-1967; writer; often referred to his Indian roots in his writings.

John Horse: born 1812; father was Seminole and his mother Black; served as advisor to Osceola in Seminole Wars; founded Wewoka, Oklahoma; fled to Mexico in 1850 but returned to serve as a Black Seminole scout.

John Langston: 1829-1897; father was a White Virginia plantation owner and mother Black and Indian slave; first Black to be elected to public office (1855); became dean of Howard University Law School; US congressman from Virginia; was great-uncle of Langston Hughes.

Edmonia Lewis: 1845-1911; mother Chippewa and father a freed Black slave; known as Wildfire; sculptor; most famous sculpture was "Cleopatra."

Bill Picket: 1863-1932; mother was Choctaw and Father Indian and Black; raised among Mexicans; inventor of bull-dogging; most wildly applauded cowboy of the period; performed with Will Rogers and Tom Mix; considered himself a Black man.

Edward Rose: born 1780; father White and his mother Black and Cherokee; fur trapper, frontiersman, linguist, interpreter and guide; helped establish good relations between trappers and Indians; became a Crow chief.

George Henry White: 1852-1918; father was a Black slave and mother was Indian and Irish; congressman from North Carolina and last former slave to serve in national legislature; identified with Black ancestors.

Quotes

"Indians have become more Black than Red."

                Thomas Jefferson, as he removed federal recognition from some tribes, early 1800's.

"To tell the truth, we don't know what the hell we is but we know we ain't niggers."

                              An Indian with African ancestry, 1870's.

"I beg you to save and not destroy these people."

             Mississippi senator and former runaway slave pleading for justice for Indians, 1870's.

"We are identical as the subject of American wrongs, outrages, and oppression, and therefore same in interest."

                Martin Delany, early Black Nationalist on the subject of Indians, early 1900's.

"One of the longest unwritten chapters of the history of the US is that treating the relations of the Negroes and Indians."

                          Carter Woodson, *Journal of Negro History*, 1920.

"I was a Cherokee slave and now I am a Cherokee freedwoman, and besides that I am a quarter Cherokee my own self. And this is the way it is"

                            Sarah Wilson, American slave narratives, 1936.

"Miss Cody is a lovely Black woman; she should focus on that heritage."

            A Navajo about Radmilla Cody, the Red-Black woman who earned the title of Ms. Navajo, 1997.

"I had a dream that all of my ancestors were lined up saying 'Remember us.' "

                             Gwen Davis, Red-Black Connection project, 1999.

"In our tribal standards, white blood is good and black blood is bad."

                      Interview with an East Coast Indian with African ancestry, 2002.

"What counts is who we are when the feathers and the tribal regalia are taken off."

                    Paul White Eagle, Chief, AhNiYvWiYa (Cherokee), 2004

E. MUSINGS

Do We Have Responsibilities as Red-Black People?
By Valena Broussard Dismukes

In the view of some, we as Red-black people carry a double burden. However, I choose to see it as a double responsibility and opportunity.

We can become educators…..

We are in a special position to educate the people with whom we come in contact about the existence of people like us, our history and culture. Sometimes it is our family members who need the education; more often it is uninformed members of the Native community.

We can be vigilant protectors of the environment…..

Our African and Native American forebears lived close to the earth and in harmony with it. There are those who say that ours is the last generation that will be able to make decisions in preserving the environment. We seem to have sacrificed important values in the pursuit of success, money, power, show and fail to take heed even to the simplest environmental mantra of "reduce, reuse, recycle." Many of the indigenous people in the USA and around the world are clinging to culture while adapting to the modern world. Their success in survival as cultural groups depends largely upon the quality of their environment, the floral and fauna, and the quality of air and water. And indeed, everyone's survival depends upon these things.

We can become civil rights activists…..

Yes, tremendous progress has been made since Indians became citizens in 1924 and since the civil rights movements of the 1960's but much remains to be done. We need to be alert to actions of the government that abridge our freedoms—economic, civil, political, and religious. Equal opportunities need to be provided for education, health services, etc. in urban communities and on reservations. Geographic location, economic status, and ethnicity should have no bearing upon the access of citizens to services. We need to question the actions of governmental agencies in their handling of suspects, legislative acts, and sacred and historic sites. We need to question the media in its handling of issues of bias and relevancy in reporting. >

We can become culture bearers…..

We need to inform ourselves of our personal family history through genealogy research and collection of oral history from our elders. We can discover the arts of our ancestors by taking workshops. We can conduct a study of the rich cultural history and language of our ancestors and bring aspects of that culture into our modern lives. We need to support cultural institutes through donations of time and money. We can share what we know with our family, especially the young ones.

We can become truth seekers…..

Many people operate on the basis of ignorance, half-truths, and even lies about many topics, especially those of Native Americans and about people of color in general. By challenging these half-truths and lies that bombard us, no matter who tells them, we can uncover facts and help alleviate irrational fears and biases.

In other words, we can become more fully human.

A Retrospective Look at the Red Road
By Asani Charles

I was once asked to write about my Red Road experience. That was some ten years ago. It is amazing how much we grow, rethink, and advance over time. Hindsight is 20-20 because our strange experiences begin to make sense only when we can look back and laugh at our *faux pas* and nod at our wise choices. Still, reflecting on this thing called the Red Road, I continue to wonder if it is a road, on a which a person travels, or instead, a daily conscious decision to be who I am without apology.

I guess you can say I had a typical Red Black childhood. My paternal Native line was kept hidden for two generations while my maternal Native line had Indian glimpses here and there. Somebody would refer to Aunt Lena and "her people" or to her brother, great grandpa Joe, the "old Indian." For the most part we were Black. It wasn't until my adult years that I saw an openness about our dual heritage evolve in the family. Naturally, I bumbled about with questions and mistakes when I first came to know the history and became a member of the American Indian community. The beautiful thing is that I was never denied. >

Humor is a godsend because it allows us to laugh while dealing with our issues. That's why I so appreciate Sherman Alexie's unique brand of Indian humor. I remember reading his article on vision quests and ominous music and finally understanding why I felt so self-conscious and inadequate when first learning about my Indianness. I had bought into many of the misconceptions about Natives because, other than the family glimpses, they were all I knew. I judged others as well as myself by ye old faithful "Dances with Wolves" standard. I sought validation for the Indian aberrations promoted by non-Indian media. For a while, I had a problem with my skin color and I expected to experience some discrimination because it wasn't Indian enough. I worried that African Americans would think I was crazy in choosing a new assimilation, "wannabeism." Over time, I did what should be natural; I got over it! I came to realize that my Indian name, a rarity within both my tribes, would have to be my South African name given to me at birth. Imagine my laughter when I learned the Zulu "Asani" is spelled exactly the same in Canadian Cree, and shares a similar affirming meaning. In South Africa, it is interpreted to mean "independence." Among the Canadian Cree, it means "strong rock." Consider this—a Red Black child given a Red Black name.

In retrospect, having always been bi-cultural and accepted as such in the Native community, I continue to hold that the Red Road is not a road for me at all. It is a consciousness of dual heritage and responsibility. I am no more on a road trip traveling through Indian Country with stops in New Ageism and Metaphysics than I would be on a bus riding to the land of Black thought and misconceptions; black sheep, black villains, etc. I recognize the power of the alliance of Red and Black people and carry unapologetic pride in both. I strive to end the cycle of silence and instill in my children the knowledge of who they are and from where they come. Perhaps the road they travel will not be an itinerary of "what am I?" but of "who will I become?"

A Wannabee
By Valena Broussard Dismukes

As I searched through federal records for a trace of my Choctaw heritage—

As I joined family discussions about the Dancing Rabbit Creek Treaty and land due us--

Some people called me a wannabee. >

As I camped at Point Conception with the Chumash to protest the Western Gate—

As I protested at Big Mountain, sitting on the floor eating lamb and zucchini stew—

Some people called me a wannabee.

As I lamented the innocent lives lost along the Trail of Tears—

As I journeyed to the mountains to join in the celebration of the seasons—

Some people called me a wannabee.

As I wore real turquoise next to my skin—

As I smudged my father's body with sage until the smoke alarm sounded—

Some people called me a wannabee.

As I worked with others to bring Black Indians together—

As I traveled to schools and meetings speaking on the Red-Black Connection—

Some people called me a wannabee.

As I celebrated the awards given to the film, "Black Indians"—

As I was feted with venison sausage by a band of Missouri Cherokees—

No one called me a wannabee.

Times are changing for Red-Black people.

The Heart Knows No Color
By Gwendolyn Davis

The goal of Black Indian people is recognition for all the "pieces of the blanket," which includes all of the indigenous peoples of this continent, put back together. This includes all the Native American descendants, whether Red, Black, Brown or White.

At some time in the past, there were ancestors of different hues who came together for preservation. These unions resulted in the family units that produced offspring of multi-ethnic origins. The bloodlines became not mixed, but united. I believe these unions produced a combination of the best of what each race has to offer the other. In the confusion of political and economic upheavals and other negative aspects of this continent's history, that unit, love and camaraderie became lost in the constant struggle to survive genocide, disenfranchisement, and identity theft. We became a people defined by someone other than ourselves.

In attempt to placate the dominant society of what had become America, we began to be at odds with each other. While we originally drew our boundaries by nations, we began to make distinctions of color. This drew a color line between us that eroded the foundation of our societies and pitted many of us against each other. In many cases, we began to disassociate ourselves from those who represented a color/racial liability in our fight to gain recognition. Somewhere along this journey called life, we began to lose our connection to each other and to the very values and cultural sameness that had brought us together in the first place.

Our struggles were much the same although the outcome took different paths. Our Red relations were either killed or forced-marched onto reservations to Indian Territory (now Oklahoma). Those who remained behind lost their land and their identity as Indians. After the Civil War, our Black relations were turned out on their own, from the bondage of the plantation system to another form of bondage, that of race and color.

Before color barriers were raised, there were many accounts of races intermixing as they all recovered from slavery and indentured servitude. While economics and survival played their parts, there was still the fact that many races came together out of mutual admiration of each other and love for each other. Yes, love. If left alone, the heart knows no color limitations.

As we come together and begin to share our heritage and accept each other for that which the Creator has made, we begin to heal. As we acknowledge and forgive each other for the past mistakes of our ancestors, we begin to mend the circle. As we pull together, pooling our strengths, each one helping to cast of the cloaks of ignorance and misconceptions about each other and ourselves, we become strong. Then, finally, our circle is mended and we become family once again as we were of old.

Narrative

By Marilyn Vann

From my youth, I was introduced to Cherokee nation history, family history, and spent time in the Cherokee nation as a youth. I learned that my ancestor, Rider Fields, a Cherokee Indian who was born in Georgia around 1800, moved to Alabama and to Indian territory on the Trail of Tears during the 1830's. When I was five years old, my father told me we were Indians with some "colored" blood. While we have oral history of Indian ancestors, we have no specific knowledge of our African ancestors. Every person with African ancestry who was born between 1907 and about 1970 in Oklahoma has it notated on their birth certificates. The State of Oklahoma defined "Negroes" as people with one drop of African ancestry. And while I do have a tribal membership card and number, I had difficulty in getting it.

Our written history includes documents showing family members on the original Dawes Commission enrollment sheets, certifying them as members of the Cherokee nation and documents showing where their land allotments are located. We also have the actual family testimonies given to the U.S. government on the issue of our Indian ancestry.

I am very involved in the tribal community in Nowata County, attending powwows, Cherokee language classes, and potluck dinners. I dance at social stomp dances (traditional dances of the Southeastern tribes such as the Cherokee, Creek, and Seminole.) I enjoy listening to powwow and stomp music.

Most long-time residents of Oklahoma have Indian ancestry. All of our friends and my family on both my parents' sides are aware of this ancestry. Some family members are current tribal members of the Cherokee, Creek, or Chickasaw nations and those family members not enrolled are descendants of tribal members. Despite this history, the occasional "stranger" with a tribal political agenda will state a belief that most people of African heritage have no Indian Blood. Except for certain political settings, one rarely hears that belief expressed to one's face.

I grew up in Ponca City, where most of the people in the neighborhood were Indian. My daughter did not have this experience nor did she spend much time in the Cherokee nation community. She has been to some cultural events such as powwows. She attended some meetings of Indian Students Association while in college in Norman, Oklahoma and is very aware of both her African and her Indian ancestry.

Currently I am involved in the struggle for Freedmen tribal rights, challenging the efforts of the Cherokee nation to remove Indians with African ancestry from voter rolls, and ultimately, from tribal rolls.

Author's Note: Marilyn Vann, an engineer of Cherokee and Chickasaw descent, is President of the Descendants of Freedman of the Five Civilized Tribes Association located in Oklahoma. She has led the battle for the protection of rights of the Cherokee Freedman as efforts have been made by the Cherokee Nation to remove the Freedmen from the tribal rolls. The Freedmen were removed from tribal citizenship in a March 2007 vote. The tribal courts reinstated in May 2007 pending appeals in the Cherokee Nation Courts and Federal courts. At the same time, the attorney for the Cherokee Nation agreed to temporarily grant citizenship rights to Freedmen while the constitutionality of the original vote is discussed in court. This controversy is ongoing.

ABOUT THE AUTHOR

Valena Broussard Dismukes (African, Choctaw, Scottish, Irish, French) worked in the Los Angeles Unified School District where she was a department head, mentor, and coordinator. While teaching, Dismukes studied photography. Since that beginning she has had numerous photographs and articles published and has participated in over fifty solo, group, and juried exhibitions. Among other awards, she received a grant to photograph the Exposition Park community during the 1984 Olympic Games in Los Angeles. "As Seen," a book of her photographs, was published in 1995. Her interest in world cultures has taken her to over forty-five countries.

Dismukes' photographs reflect her continuing fascination with people that is fueled by extensive travels abroad. In appreciation of traditional artists and their work, she has filled her home with ethnic baskets, dolls, and textiles.

Dismukes has lectured and appeared on radio and television discussing Black Indians. Her major photographic essay, "Native Americans: The Red-Black Connection," upon which this book is based, has been featured at thirteen museums, galleries, and libraries across the country. Photographs from this series are part of the award-winning film by Rich-Heape Films, Inc., *Black Indians: An American Story*.

She was a co-founder of African Native Americans of Southern California (ANASCA) and is a member of Neskinukat, a California Native Artists network. Dismukes volunteers weekly at Haramokngna, an intertribal American Indian Cultural Center in the San Gabriel Mountains of Southern California.

RED-BLACK CONNECTION
Contemporary Urban African-Native Americans
and Their Stories of Dual Indentity
Valena Broussard Dismukes

You can order additional books with this order form, online at Dismukes.myexpose.com, Amazon.com, or through your independent bookstore. For additional information, contact the author at vdismukes@netzero.net.

Please send me ____ copy(ies) of **THE RED-BLACK CONNECTION**. I am enclosing my check/money order for $24.95, plus $3.50 shipping and handling, for each copy. (California residents add 8.25% sales tax.)

No cash, credit cards, or COD's. Allow 2-4 weeks for delivery.

PLEASE PRINT CLEARLY

Name:

Street Address:

City/State/Zip: Phone:

Send order to:

Grace Enterprises

c/o Valena Broussard Dismukes

3800 Stocker Street, Suite 1

Los Angeles, CA 90008